The Leprechaun Trap

Dedicated to Angela

The Leprechaun Trap

By David and Kelly Clinch
Illustrations by Valerie Bouthyette

Published 2008 by Clinch Media
© 2008 Text Clinch Media, Atlanta Georgia
© 2008 Illustrations, Valerie Bouthyette

All rights reserved under U.S. and Pan-American Copyright Convention.
No part of this publication may be reproduced without the prior written permission
of the copyright holder with the exception of brief quotations appearing in reviews.

ISBN 0-9800835-0-8

ISBN 978-0-9800835-0-7

Library of Congress Control Number: 2008901259

Visit our webpage at www.TheLeprechaunTrap.com

Every year at the beginning of March, the little leprechaun doll magically appeared, sitting innocently on the foot of Emma's bed. The children guessed that he had come to them from Ireland—perhaps sneaking into Granny's suitcase on one of her many visits from Dublin—and they had named him Liam.

Once Liam arrived, the children knew they would wake up each morning to discover half-eaten potatoes on the kitchen floor, or the cereal boxes spilled open on the counter-top, or sprinkles of shamrock on the breakfast table—their little leprechaun doll sitting in the middle of it all, "asleep" once again until the next night.

Daddy told the children they were lucky to have a leprechaun in their house because if they could catch a leprechaun causing mischief on Saint Patrick's Day, they had a chance of stealing his gold. But try as they might, the children could never catch Liam.

And this year was proving no different. Emma woke up on the first of March to find Liam sitting on her bed, a twinkle in his eye. She grinned and yelled to Patrick and her baby sister, Molly, "The leprechaun is back!"

"Again?" said Patrick, running in to see the doll. "Then we had better start working on another plan to catch him right away. I really want his gold this time."

"Yay! I love plans!" said little Molly, who was only three. But then, after thinking a moment, she asked, "Why do we need a plan? What's a leprechaun?"

Emma let Molly hold the doll and reminded her that Liam was a magic little fellow. He visited them in March every year and awakened every night until Saint Patrick's Day to cause trouble in their house. Emma, who was ten, had been trying to catch the leprechaun for as long as she could remember.

"Daddy says Liam is lucky, but I think he's just trouble!" said Patrick, who was seven and had built his first leprechaun trap when he was only two. "He looks harmless now, but you just wait and see, Molly. Even if we lock him up in a cupboard or tie him to the bed before we go to sleep, he always gets away when he wakes up, and then he's even naughtier!"

Patrick looked down at Liam and added, "If we don't capture him this Saint Patrick's Day, he'll keep coming back every year to make even bigger messes, and we'll never get his gold!"

"Daddy thinks that Liam feels homesick for Ireland," said Emma. "He says leprechauns should be in Ireland making shoes for the fairies and earning gold, not here in America causing trouble. Daddy always says the leprechaun is very cute!"

Molly hugged the doll and smiled. "I think he's cute, too!" she said.

"No, silly," replied Emma, "that doesn't mean he's cute like a puppy! In Ireland 'cute' means he's very clever and naughty. Remember Molly, Daddy says Saint Patrick's Day is the only day anyone can ever catch a naughty leprechaun."

"And that…" said Patrick with a very serious look on his face "…is why we need a plan."

As usual, the trouble began immediately after Liam arrived. One morning, the children woke to find Patrick's feet tied to his bed post, and Liam holding the string.

The next night they tried putting Liam in the toy box and piling heavy books on top to keep him from getting out, but the following morning…

… they found all the water in the toilets turned green, and Liam napping in the bathtub. They tried locking him in the pantry one night, but the next day …

… their dog, Murphy, had green footprints all over him. Liam was sitting in the dog crate,

holding a paint brush from Molly's art set, still as a stone, asleep again.

The day before Saint Patrick's Day, Emma called a meeting in the playroom. "We have GOT to do something!" she cried. "The trouble is getting worse! And we've only got one day to catch him!"

"But what kind of trap should we make?" asked Patrick, "None of the traps we've made before have ever worked."

"Well, we're just going to have to come up with something better," Emma answered, dumping out all the pictures of past years. "There has to be SOMETHING we haven't tried."

"Last year, we tried putting a potato for him to eat at the bottom of a big box, hoping he would fall in, remember that?" said Patrick.

"Yes," said Emma, holding up that photo. "Look at the big mess he made then -- the kitchen was destroyed! Chairs were on the table, the trash was turned over and Liam was GONE!"

"Here's the year we left some Irish bacon in a mouse trap. Remember we found one of his little shoes stuck in the trap the next morning. He even dropped a few gold coins!" added Patrick. "We almost had him that year!" Molly peered curiously at the photo.

"I remember," said Emma as she found the next photo, "and I remember that mess, too! He wrote 'You can't catch me!' on the windows and disappeared!"

"Was Mommy mad at him?" asked Molly, her freckled nose all scrunched up. "Yes, really mad!" Patrick replied. He remembered Mommy washing windows all morning.

"Well, we've tried Irish food, music, and even shamrock," said Emma as they looked at all the photos. "I give up."

"Maybe he would like an Irish fairy?" said Molly.

"Don't be silly, Molly. Where would we get an Irish fairy?" exclaimed Patrick.

"Hey, wait a minute," said Emma. "That might not be a bad idea. Molly, go get the doll that Grandpa bought you when we were visiting in Dublin." Molly, who was excited to be included, scuttled up the stairs and headed for her bedroom, dragging her blanket behind her.

"What are you planning, Emma?" asked Patrick.

"Well he's homesick for Ireland…he wants to make shoes for the fairies again…why don't we give him what he wants…an Irish fairy that needs some shoes! Molly and I will dress up the Irish doll to look like a fairy and take off her shoes," said Emma.

"And I will make the trap," added Patrick, snickering.

"Exactly," said Emma, "just make it a good one this time!"

Molly ran into the playroom, beaming and holding up her Irish doll. "Here she is! Did I have a good idea?"

"Yes, you did," said Emma, "now let's get busy."

That night, the night before Saint Patrick's Day, the children stayed up late making and setting the trap.

Molly and Emma made the doll look like an Irish fairy who had lost her shoes. Now, the children had never seen an Irish fairy, even though they had visited Ireland many times, but they were pretty sure that Irish fairies did not have wings. Instead, they made a beautiful dress for her from green and white silk, carefully cutting it to fit just right. Then Emma placed a bit of Irish cheese on a tiny dish from her old tea set on one side of the fairy and a sprinkle of shamrock on the other.

Patrick built a small house out of Popsicle sticks for the fairy to sit in and covered it with leaves, since Daddy had told them that Irish fairies always live under bushes. Then Molly painted a rainbow on the door of the house with her art set because she remembered Daddy saying that leprechauns always keep their gold in a pot at the end of a rainbow.

Finally, Patrick found a small bag of dirt he had collected when they climbed Croagh Patrick Mountain in Ireland last summer, and he piled that up in front of the fairy as well.

"He will smell Ireland and won't be able to resist coming in," grinned Patrick, smoothing his hand across the pile of dirt. "When he steps inside to look at the fairy, he'll trip over this string underneath the dirt," he explained, "and then the door here will fall from the top of the house and trap him inside." They tested the trap again and again with Patrick's action figures playing the part of the leprechaun and finally were satisfied with their work.

"If we catch him, I'm keeping all his gold," said Patrick. He looked proudly at his creation, placing it carefully on the kitchen table for Liam to find.

Emma, Patrick, and Molly fell into bed, exhausted from all their hard work, but sure they finally had a good chance of catching Liam and winning his gold. "You just need a little bit of Irish luck," offered Daddy as he kissed them goodnight.

"You will all need some of that if I find another huge mess in the house like last year!" Mommy added, laughing.

"What are you going to do with all that gold if you catch him? That's what I want to know," asked Daddy.

"Can I share it with my friends?" asked Molly, her tired eyes half closed.

"Of course you can," answered Daddy. Mommy tucked Molly's covers tight around her and turned off the light.

Patrick was the first one up in the morning. "No feet tied to the bed," he thought to himself hopefully as he jumped up and headed for the stairs.

"No green toilet water!" shouted Emma, running past the bathroom in the hall.

Molly scrambled down the stairs after them. "Wait for me!" she called.

"Uh-oh!" said Patrick as he turned into the kitchen.

"What is it?" asked Emma. And then she turned the corner herself. "Oh no!" she exclaimed, her jaw dropping open. Molly ran into the kitchen and stopped. Her eyes opened wide and she screamed, "Daddy, come quickly!!"

The first thing they saw was the poor little fairy hanging upside down from the ceiling fan, spinning round and round, the string from the trap wrapped tightly around her. The dish that had been filled with cheese now lay broken on the floor. Beside it sat the milk container, filled with bright green milk and bits of shamrock. "I'm not drinking that!" declared Emma in disgust.

The flour and sugar containers were strewn on their sides on the counter, little green footprints running in circles through the white mess, as though their leprechaun had danced a jig in the snow. Every single drawer and cupboard in the kitchen stood open, knives and forks and pots and pans were scattered everywhere! Green glitter shone from the floor and a few gold coins were sprinkled about. The trap itself looked like a tornado had hit it—a tangle of wood, dirt, torn-up leaves, and shreds of silk from the fairy's dress was all that remained.

And there was no sign of Liam anywhere.

Then they heard barking and yelping from the laundry room. Murphy ran into the kitchen with a bright green sign attached to his tail. Emma yanked it off, and Molly gave Murphy a hug.

"What does it say?" asked Patrick.

"It says 'See you next year!'" Emma answered. "We didn't catch him!"

Daddy walked around the kitchen with the video camera, filming the damage when Mommy came into the room. She just stood there for a minute with her hands on her hips.

"I think Mommy's mad," Molly whispered.

"This has got to stop!" declared Mommy, looking around the room at the destruction. "No more leprechaun traps!"

"Don't blame us, Mommy!" said Patrick "Liam's the one who made the mess!"

"Don't worry." Daddy put down the camera and gave Mommy a big hug. "We'll clean it up…and then we'll all go out for a great big Irish breakfast. How about that?"

The children cheered. Emma started picking up bits of the broken dish while Patrick and Molly closed cupboards and drawers.

"We almost caught him. I was sure it was going to work this time," mumbled Patrick, sweeping up the last of the dirt from the floor and slipping two gold coins into his pocket for his collection.

"Can I try the green milk?" asked Molly. She tried to lift up the container to take a sip.

"No! Who knows what's in there!" Mommy grumbled. She grabbed the milk away from Molly and poured it down the sink.

Daddy smiled as he pulled the fairy doll down from the ceiling fan and untangled her from the string.

"That leprechaun is cuter than I thought," he said.

HOW TO BUILD PATRICK'S TRAP

Please visit **www.TheLeprechaunTrap.com** for more information about building your own traps and to send in your own suggestions for catching leprecauns.

NOTE: But if you have captured a leprechaun, please be **extremely careful!**

29847179R00023

Made in the USA
Middletown, DE
04 March 2016